So Who Says I Have 2ACT My Age?

Early Teen Devotionals
by Kevin Johnson

Can I Be a Christian Without Being Weird?

Why Is God Looking For Friends?

Who Should I Listen To?

Why Can't My Life Be a Summer Vacation?

So Who Says I Have to Act My Age?

So Who Says I Have 2 ACT My Age?

KEVIN JOHNSON

BETHANY HOUSE PUBLISHERS
MINNEAPOLIS, MINNESOTA 55438

Published by Bethany House Publishers
A Ministry of Bethany Fellowship, Inc.
11300 Hampshire Avenue South
Minneapolis, Minnesota 55438

Printed in the United States of America

Library of Congress Cataloging-in-Publication Data

Johnson, Kevin (Kevin Walter)
   So who says I have to act my age? / Kevin Johnson.
      p. cm.

    1. Teenagers—Prayer-books and devotions—English.
2. Teenagers—Conduct of life. I. Title.
BV4850.J645   1994
242'.63—dc20   94–25137
ISBN 1–55661–414–4 (pbk.)   CIP
                                      AC

To Dad and Mom
Roy and Lois Johnson
for helping me grow up

KEVIN JOHNSON is an associate pastor at Elmbrook Church in metro Milwaukee, where he works with almost 400 sixth–eighth graders. While his training includes a M.Div. from Fuller Theological Seminary and a B.A. in English and Print Journalism from the University of Wisconsin at River Falls, his current interests run along the lines of cycling, in-line skating, books, guitar, and shortwave radio. Kevin and his wife, Lyn, live in Wisconsin with their two children, Nathaniel and Karin.

Contents

Part 3: Playin' Smart

Part 4: Steerin' Straight

PART 1

BUILDIN'

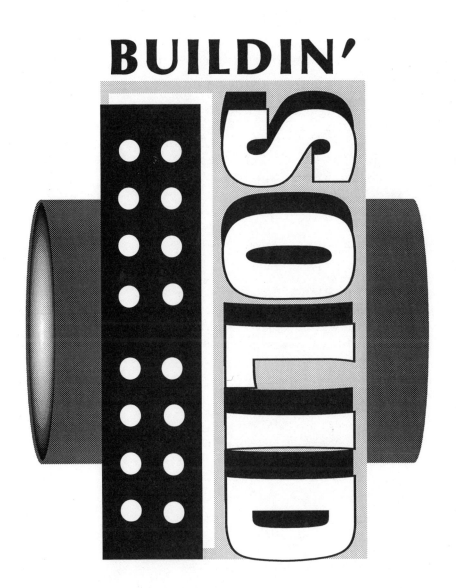

SOLID

1

Escape From the Little Table

Grandparents, aunts, uncles, and cousins crowd your kitchen, anxious to sit down for Thanksgiving dinner. Your mom points to you and your eight-year-old sister and your six-year-old twin cousins: ". . . and you all sit over there."

"Over there" is an orange plastic picnic table brought in to seat the kiddies. You struggle to squeeze your knees underneath. *Why am I always stuck at the little table?*

" . . . In Christ's name we pray," your dad finishes. "Amen."

Your eyes open to see the flash of a spud-loaded spoon wielded by your cousin Joshua.

"Incoming!" his sister squeals as they both let spoonfuls fly.

Splat. Potatoes in your hair. Stuck to your eyebrows. Glopping off your nose. All over your shirt.

"Joshua Andrew! Mandi Elizabeth!" your aunt barks before you can lunge at them. "Time out—on the steps—NOW!" Big trouble—she used their middle names. This should be good.

Your aunt, however, calms herself when she notices everyone staring at *her* instead of at your cousins. She shifts everyone's attention to you.

"You know, you wouldn't want to be seen wearing

those potatoes," she says as she hands you a towel. "They don't go with your shirt." You roll your eyes.

Your mom shakes her head as she looks you up and down. "What did you do to start *that*?" she asks.

"Mom, I didn't do anything," you protest. "Can I pound those brats?"

"Act your age," she reminds you. "Maybe it's time you move up to the big table," she suggests. "Grab your plate and we'll squeeze in a chair next to mine."

It's just as bad at the adult table. Boring. The dads debate the merits of purchasing the family minivan versus leasing. *Who cares?* you think. Everyone oohs and aahs over the asparagus. "Oh, thanks," your mom blushes. "It's so good when it's fresh from the garden." *Get a life. All of you!* An older cousin who had already graduated to the big table giggles and whispers to her boyfriend. You worry that they're talking about you. After dinner she flops her head on his shoulder. *Gag!*

You ask to be excused to go outside. On your way out you pick up an olive and squish it in your little cousin's ear.

"Say anything and I'll clobber you," you whisper to him.

And you wish that maybe you could go back to the little table.

If you goof off like a little kid they shake their finger: "You're not a three-year-old, you know. Act your age." If you try to act older they shake in their shoes: "You're not ready for that. Act your age."

So what *is* your age? And who says how you should act?

God knows. He knew you well when you were a kid. He counts on being close to you when you're an adult. And He wants you to stick next to Him when you feel stuck between tables.

This book is meant to help you hear what God has to say to you right now—while you dangle in that cool time of life between diapers and dentures. Read a chapter at a sitting, one a day if you can. Bring a Bible that's easy to read so you can look up the passages where it says ✔ **Read**. You can hear more of what God wants to say to you by flipping to the other passages that pop up here and there in parentheses. Each chapter finishes with a verse you might want to memorize.

God wants you to make it to the big table.

He knows you're not a baby. And He doesn't plan to make you a bore.

2

It's No Crime to Be Young

They might as well have torn down the store. The hangout was gone.

Old Mr. Robinson owned a quickmart next to the middle school. He always said that he liked kids, which to him meant anyone under forty.

But students were his favorites. He knew most of them, even the ones who tried to rip him off before they figured out he was all right. When kids had problems at school or at home, they stuck around to talk with Mr. Robinson.

One day Mr. Robinson told his friends he was retiring and selling the store.

Things changed fast. To the new owner, "student" meant "shoplifter." Everyone was guilty until proven innocent. Trying to guard the cash register and the candy aisle at the same time flustered the new owner, so he hung a sign on the door: *Only one student in the store at a time*. When kids still bunched on the sidewalk in front of the store he blasted elevator music through a loudspeaker to push them away.

So they left.

Read Mark 10:13–16. If Jesus owned a store would He chase students away?

It was like going to get an autograph from a megastar, only better. Parents brought their children to Je-

15

sus for Him to "bless" them, to put His hands on their heads and proclaim God's kindness and love for them. Get the picture straight: Some kids swarming Jesus were small enough for Him to pick up, but not all. (The word Mark wrote here for "children" is used in Luke 8:42 to mean a twelve-year-old.)

The kids and young teens closing in on Jesus didn't even get close. Jesus' friends—His disciples—blasted them away: "Don't waste His time," or "He has things to do. People to see. All more important than you."

Jesus stopped His disciples and blasted *them*. Kids were exactly the people He wanted to see—not because kids are constantly cute or nonstop nice or because they always act the way God wants, but because they demonstrate how to depend on God. People need to accept God's love the way a son or daughter accepts a parent's love.

The only way to make sense of God is to think like a kid.

But when Jesus saw what was happening he was very much displeased with his disciples and said to them, "Let the children come to me, for the Kingdom of God belongs to such as they.
Don't send them away!"

MARK 10:14, TLB

3

Do These Belong to Anyone?

You can still picture your teacher waving a pair of underwear high overhead. "Class, do these belong to anyone?"

Your fourth-grade class was field tripping to the middle school pool and you had been terrified—of the locker rooms, showers, changing in front of other kids. So you hatched a plan. You wore your swimsuit to school under your clothes, and hid your underwear— along with an enormous towel to change underneath— in a duffel. You had everything covered.

You snickered. *What doof would drop a pair of underwear in front of the whole class?* Mrs. Burzloff kept waving the underwear, as if to flag down the owner. *What's she going to do next? Wear them on her head?*

Then you recognized them. You checked your duffel. They were yours.

☑ **Read Psalm 139:13–16. You look in the mirror and hardly recognize yourself. What's going on?**

You might still wish you could change in a locker. What you feel, how you think, or who you see in the mirror may be bewildering or embarrassing or confusing.

You're like a video image morphing from one creature into another. You know who you used to be. Now you only catch a glimpse of yourself, in mid-morph motion.

The biggest unknown is what you're turning into. A werewolf? A beluga whale? A not-so-jolly giant? Or maybe someone is playing a cruel joke on you and you're never going to grow up.

Your Designer isn't worried or confused. God made you unique, just the way He wanted. God made your "inward being"—your brain and feelings. He "knit together" a cover for you—your body. That makes you "fearful" and "wonderful"—not scary, but awestriking and incredible.

God has been caring for you since He put you together in your mom's womb. He has you—body, brain, and heart—figured out ("the days ordained for me"). And what He plans for you is good (Jeremiah 29:11).

For you created my inmost being; you knit me together in my mother's womb. I praise you because I am fearfully and wonderfully made; your works are wonderful, I know that full well.

PSALM 139:13–14

4

Size Twelve

"Hoooo-weeeeee!" Jason's golfer bellowed. "Look at that! Never seen anything like it."

The foursome of golfers and their caddies all whistled through their teeth at the sight of the third hole. Rain had made the whole fairway a water hazard. Everyone mumbled about skipping to the next hole, but Jason's golfer teed up and composed himself to whack the ball.

"Don't worry about it, gents," he said. "Haven't you seen the size of my caddie's feet? Hey kid—what size shoe do you wear?"

"Twelve."

"Canoes! Just what I guessed. You can float out to fetch golf balls."

▶ **Read 1 Samuel 16:1–13. What matters most about a person?**

It feels as if all anyone notices is how you look on the outside. Everyone makes fun of your feet. Everyone stares at your nose. They all think you're a clod because they saw you trip when you walked up the steps.

So guys stare in the mirror and flex their muscles and wonder if the girls think they're manly. Girls flex their legs so their thighs *splurrggge* a half inch less.

19

God is interested in more than that. When God sent Samuel to find a king, Samuel was wowed by Eliab, Jesse's oldest son. God told Samuel to look deeper. When God signaled that little brother David was to be king, it turned out that David wasn't current president of the local chapter of Uglies Unanimous. He was a shepherd, tan and strong.

But the tone of his skin wasn't the most important thing about him. God knew that David's heart was what made David ready to be king.

You achieve real hunkhood or babedom not when you're toned and tanned on the outside but when your insides are well-developed—when you're self-controlled, honest, unselfish, thoughtful and thinking, when you respect God, yourself, and others.

Being ugly on the inside is what makes you a reject.

"Do not consider his appearance or his height, for I have rejected him. The LORD *does not look at the things man looks at. Man looks at the outward appearance, but the* LORD *looks at the heart."*

1 SAMUEL 16:7B

5

Burst That Bubble

Jamie's head had blown into a big snot bubble ever since she got her driver's license.

"*Please?*" Rebecca begged. "Just to the mall. It's just me and Natalie."

"Not with us! Ride your bikes. Melissa and I are taking the car by ourselves."

"Dad!" Rebecca howled. "Jamie won't give us a ride to the mall."

"Jamie, give Becca a ride or *you* won't be taking the car."

Rebecca and Natalie jumped into the backseat. Jamie snarled at them. "I'm giving you a ride because Dad said I had to. When we get to the mall I'm dropping you off and we're going to the other end. Stay out of our way. We don't want to be seen with you twerps."

✔ Read 2 Timothy 2:19–22. What does it mean to be mature?

You would call it your lucky day if some older brothers and sisters cared as much about you as the family dog. Parents can seem as if they've forgotten what it's like to be your age. And teachers often assume you won't be issued a brain until you turn thirty.

What do *they* know that you don't, anyway? Some seem so stupid.

You're right. A driver's license means someone can safely operate a car, not a mouth. A high school or college diploma doesn't guarantee a person has graduated from the terrible twos. Maturity is more than having car and house payments and piling up birthdays.

So when the Bible urges you to become mature by being "made holy," like God—who's *reeeally* old—the thrill might not pump your bike tires.

God may be *reeeally* old, but more He's also *reeeeeeeally* cool. And acting like Him is the secret to real life. Maturity is being what God wants you to be when He wants you to be it. It's becoming like Him in your attitudes and actions.

When you grow in obedience to your Master, running away from what's wrong and chasing what's right, then you're "an instrument for noble purposes," ready for the best God has for you (Ephesians 2:10).

That's choosing to be precious gold, not a stump or a lump. Or a snot bubble.

————————

If a man cleanses himself from the latter, he will be an instrument for noble purposes, made holy, useful to the Master and prepared to do any good work.

2 TIMOTHY 2:21

6
Guess I'll Keep Them

The tackle was clean and hard.

It looked as if a refrigerator had dropped on Nate and swallowed him up. When the pile cleared, Nate still lay pretzel-shaped on the field.

In the stands his parents could see something was wrong. When Nate didn't get up, his coach ran in from the sideline. Nate writhed in pain, his leg broken.

"Where's my dad?" Nate cried as they took him off the field. "Get my dad and mom!"

Since the day you were born your parents have been letting go—little by little allowing you to grow more independent. Once they held your hand wherever you went. Now they're content to watch you from the stands.

Sometimes you're glad to spot them in the front row. Other times you want them to get lost at the snack table.

But they're the first ones who come running when you need them.

And they're probably the people you want the most.

▶ **Read Luke 2:40–52. Did Jesus ever struggle with His parents?**

Jesus never sinned (Hebrews 4:15). He never strayed from God's plan, never disobeyed God's commands. That doesn't mean He never perplexed Ma and Pa.

It wasn't as if the Joseph Carpenter family of Nazareth drove off and forgot twelve-year-old Jesus at a rest area. Joseph didn't glance in the backseat and turn to Mary and say, "Have you seen Jesus? Whoops!" Traveling to the Passover Feast caravan style, Joseph and Mary assumed Jesus was elsewhere in the crowd, probably with His friends or cousins. It sounds as if it took a day to realize He was gone, a day to travel back, and a day to search. What a pain!

Jesus was fine. He wasn't sleeping on a sewer grate or spray-painting graffiti on camels. That wasn't the point.

Mary and Joseph knew it was their job for a few more years to keep track of their son. And Jesus knew He still needed His parents. He went home.

. . . His mother said to him, "Son, why have you treated us like this? Your father and I have been anxiously searching for you." . . . Then he went down to Nazareth with them and was obedient to them.

LUKE 2:48B, 51A

7

We Don't Want
No Farmer Tans

You used to be such a nerd. Until you became a Wedunnawannafammatanna, that is.

At the beginning you didn't even know what a 'Tanna was. You were totally tugged toward a group with jungle-print surfboards and coordinated swim-suits. They lay on the beach. They didn't say much. Just things like "Whoa, dude." Seemed serene.

You found out that 'Tannas didn't bathe. And they chain-smoked funny little cigarettes rolled fresh from weeds. "I don't do it myself," you told people who worried about your new friends. "They're melding their minds toward universal peace. It's so cool. They see stuff." No doubt.

You start reevaluating your friendships when your skin blisters and sprouts suspicious pre-cancerous growths, and then your hair gets gnarly and gnatted and you gnotice you can't get a comb through it. Bad scene.

☑ **Read Genesis 37:1–11. When is it good to be different?**

What a jerk! It was bad enough that Joseph thought his family would bow to him. But he couldn't keep his thoughts to himself. Joseph's older brothers decided to kill the dreamer, but it paid better to sell him as a slave (Genesis 37:12–36).

A jerk? Check again: Joseph thought for himself. He spoke out, regardless of what others thought of him. He wanted to stand apart from his brothers, to lead, to be more than a seventeen-year-old shooing sheep.

Years after he became a slave, God allowed Joesph to predict seven years of bad crops. He rose to power when he helped the Egyptians store food and avoid starvation. When his brothers had to go to Egypt to scrounge food they bowed before a great ruler who fed them, who turned out to be Joseph, the brother they were sure they had done in (Genesis 45).

Joseph realized then that God hadn't made him different and given him power to pay back his brothers. It was so he could play a part in God's plans.

God wants you to think hard about how He can use you—to do right at school, to tell teammates about Him, to reach out and feed the homeless, teach kids to read, or help the elderly do what they can't do anymore.

Dream big about what God wants you to be.

Not to be strange. Not to be selfish. But to be significant for God.

Joseph had a dream. . . .

GENESIS 37:5A

8
Whacky World

The argument got so ugly that everyone in the hall stopped to listen.

"You're acting like a baby," Shawna spit.

"Really? Well, you *are* a baby," Ginny laughed nastily.

Shawna gulped. "What are you talking about?"

"You know what I'm talking about," Ginny shot back. "You're a baby. You still wet the bed."

That was the secret Ginny had sworn never, *ever* to tell. Shawna and Ginny met in third grade, and Shawna stayed over at Ginny's house a couple times a month. She always brought blankets and sheets instead of a sleeping bag. Some weekends Shawna had to toss her bedding in the wash or take stuff home in a plastic bag.

The girls were best friends. Shawna's problem didn't matter.

Until now.

Read Luke 22:47–54. How did Jesus react when Peter whacked off a guard's ear with a knife?

With a kiss for a greeting, Judas—one of Jesus' twelve handpicked followers—showed the guards which man was Jesus.

Peter watched, horrified. For three years he had followed Jesus. He was one of Jesus' three closest friends. Now his friend and master was being seized by soldiers, torn away to be tried and to die. Peter was terrified and angry.

He lashed out (John 18:10). It felt like the thing to do.

Your emotions say it's right, so you do it. A teacher gives you extra homework and you cuss under your breath. You slam your bedroom door in anger at your parents. You feel hurt and end a friendship. You see something you like so you take it.

But all the emotions that swirl inside of you—anger, excitement, hatred, jealous, boredom, laziness—can't tell you right from wrong. Your sure guide is the Bible, with its calm, unchanging commands (Psalm 19:7–11).

"No more of this!" Jesus says. So think—don't just feel—before you act. Jesus isn't always around to reattach the ears you whack off.

But Jesus answered, "No more of this!" And he touched the man's ear and healed him.

LUKE 22:51

9
Life Is a Logroll

A year ago when his mom remarried, Matt expected his life to stay put for a while. His biological father had started drinking again, so Matt decided to move in with Mom and her new husband. He hated switching schools, but it got him out of his father's yelling range. Besides, his mom's new husband had a pretty nice place.

Then last Tuesday his mom sat him down. "Joe and I are getting a divorce," his mom told him. "Things aren't working out. You and I will need to pack our stuff and find an apartment. We need to be out within a week."

"We're staying around here, aren't we?" Matt protested. He was sick of school shuffling.

"I don't know. I think Joe and I need some space. You understand, don't you?"

Sure. I always understand.

☑ **Read Hebrews 13:8. What one thing in life stays the same when everything else changes?**

Life swirls: You switch schools. You move. Your mom might go to work and dad might lose his job. Your classes, schedule, and teachers never stay the same. Your world changes: Neighborhoods spring up. Malls multiply. TV shows premier and fizzle. You find a new favorite song. And besides that, *you* change: Your brain and body expand. You cut your hair and buy new clothes. You swap friends. You start a job. Your interests and hobbies and after-school activities come and go.

So even if your family isn't lurching, you still may feel as if you're logrolling. Life shifts, spins, and bobs, threatening your balance and leaving you insecure and powerless. Sometimes you give up and go in the drink.

Jesus never changes. Yesterday He showed himself to be God on earth (John 1:14). Today He's the one who won't leave you (Hebrews 13:5). And He prepares a forever home for you (John 14:3).

Jesus doesn't always stop the log spinning. But if you ask for His help He climbs on the log, holds your hand, puts cleats on your feet, and helps you dance.

And when life flips you into the water He'll pull you back up on the log.

---

*Jesus Christ is the same yesterday
and today and forever.*

HEBREWS 13:8

10

Game Master

"Breakfast was great, Mrs. Dahmke." Julie groaned. "I'm stuffed. Thanks for letting me stay over."

"Thanks for coming, Julie," Nicole's mom answered. "It sounds like you two had a good time. Say, I'll need to take you home now because I have errands to run."

Julie whispered to Nicole. "But it's Saturday! Don't you want to watch videos or something? Then we could go to the mall."

"Sure, but Mom says she needs to take you *now*."

"I don't want to go. I always make sure I'm not home on Saturday mornings so I don't have to do my chores. My brother will do them. He's so juvenile."

"You *what*?" Nicole was amazed. "If I tried that my parents would never let me out of the house!"

▶ **Read Matthew 25:14–30. What does God expect you to do with what He gives you?**

You don't get to play ball without practicing, to have friends over without picking up, or to be part of a family without doing your part. You can't split responsibility and privilege.

Jesus said His Father's Kingdom is like a master who trusts his servants with astronomical amounts of

31

money—not a middle schooler's measly allowance but more cash than you'll touch in your life, unless you can hit homers, or skate a triple axel. Two servants work to increase the money entrusted to them. The master gives them even grander opportunities.

Yippy skippy. You do well, you get more work. Sounds like school.

Not quite. The servants hear their master's approval. They "share their master's happiness." Get it? It's like reaching the next level in a video game.

A third servant refuses to take risks. He hides what he has. He's tossed out.

God has given you vast riches, a lifetime to give back to Him what He's given you. So how much do you have? What do you have? How can you wisely invest your life to serve God?

You have the next few years to figure that out. It's all part of the fun.

His master replied, "Well done, good and faithful servant! You have been faithful with a few things; I will put you in charge of many things. Come and share your master's happiness."

MATTHEW 25:21

11

Wheeling the Wrong Way

Sheri wanted everything perfect for her date. She puckered up to the mirror to get her lipstick right, then stepped back to check her outfit. *Just right.* She looked a lot older than she was. *My mother would hate this—if she bothered to notice.*

Sheri heard Darren pull in the driveway. Sheri hated the stunts Darren did with her on the back of his motorcycle, but she figured a few seconds of terror was worth the attention he gave her.

Sheri ran outside. She hopped on, hung on, and hoped.

📫 **Read Romans 8:38–39. How do you find real acceptance?**

Trying to grow up too quick is like jumping on the backseat of a motorcycle heading fast and far the wrong way. Once you're on it's not easy to get off.

Some kids fly down dead-end roads in their attempt to grow up—smoking, drinking, inhaling, popping to feel cool; thinking they can get along without their parents; purging food or starving themselves; dating or hanging out with older kids. They push past the speed limit, thinking they can outrun the consequences of their actions.

But here's the surprise: We've *all* headed away from

God (Romans 3:10–12). We've tried to act grown-up—
too grown-up—trying to get along without God's close-
ness or commands, doing life our own way to feel big,
strong, and independent.

There's a better way to feel important. In Christ,
God offers us more love and acceptance and signifi-
cance than we can ever make for ourselves. *Nothing* is
bigger than God's love for us in Christ.

God says we deserve to ride off and never return, to
be permanently distanced from himself. That's death
(Romans 6:23). God could have said, "Have it your way.
Have a nice trip." Instead Jesus died in our place so we
could come back to Him.

We need to stop trying to be something we're not.
We can say, "God, I'm not all grown-up. I never will be.
I need you, but each day I sin. I don't live the way you
want. I accept Christ's death for my sins. I want to
follow and obey you because you love me. I'll never out-
grow you."

That's how you get off the bike and accept God's
forgiveness, a ride back home.

----

*For I am convinced that neither death nor life,
neither angels nor demons, neither the present nor
the future, nor any powers, neither height nor depth,
nor anything else in all creation, will be able to
separate us from the love of God that is in Christ
Jesus our Lord.*

ROMANS 8:38–39

12

They Call This Home?

"When are we going to leave?" Brent whispered not-too-quietly to his parents. He didn't get an answer—other than "*SHHHhh!*"

Brent loved Grandpa. Funeral homes gave him the creeps.

Brent got the message that he wasn't going anywhere, so he went back by the casket. Everyone remarked that Grandpa looked the best he had in years. Brent thought he looked like an old mannequin with its cracks and chipped paint puttied over.

In fact, everything in the place seemed unreal. Warbly church music played in the background as ladies cried on cue and men shook hands and talked baseball. Brent's little cousins darted in and out of the flowers around the casket. At the side the funeral director wore a well-rehearsed look of polite concern. He glanced at his watch a lot.

This isn't Grandpa, Brent thought as he looked back in the casket. He wondered where the real Grandpa was. He worried how it would feel to be in Grandpa's place.

📭 **Read John 14:1–7. What will the end of your life be like?**

It's scary. You don't just grow up. You grow old. Your skin wrinkles, your brain skips, and your body breaks.

And you don't just grow old. You die.

But God stays with you if you reside in a nursing home (Isaiah 46:3–4). Even a funeral home or cemetery isn't your final resting place. Christians have a better home.

When Jesus told His followers that He was "leaving" soon (John 13:33) He said not to worry. He was going to prepare a mansion for them. He knew His followers would arrive safely because He would come back for them (1 Thessalonians 4:13–17).

His disciples said *Huh?* Jesus was a carpenter, sure enough, capable of building a house. But when had He gotten into real estate? They hadn't strolled through any subdivisions to spot lots. What was He talking about?

Jesus had in mind a more lasting building— heaven. His disciples already had directions how to get there. *Jesus* was the path. And the Father would welcome them in His mansion because they knew His Son, the true and living way to God.

Heaven is your forever home. And death on earth is just the door.

———————

"Do not let your hearts be troubled. Trust in God; trust also in me. In my Father's house are many rooms. . . . I am going there to prepare a place for you."

JOHN 14:1–2

PART 2

13

She's Ki Nda Kyut

"Don't look," Mitch nudged Ryan. "She's after you again."

Ryan knew exactly who "she" was: Ki Nda Kyut, a new student at school. Wherever Ryan went, Ki Nda was there grinning at him.

"She wants to marry you," Mitch bugged. Ryan slugged.

Ki Nda did stare at Ryan a lot. Ryan didn't mind. Then rumors flew that Ryan liked Ki Nda Kyut. *That* Ryan minded. "You have to ditch her," Mitch warned him. "Don't you know that no one likes her? Everyone likes her sister, Ree Li."

So one day when Ki Nda was trailing him to class he yelled at her. "Quit following me!" Ki Nda ran off crying. She never looks at Ryan anymore.

But Ryan still thinks she's kind of cute.

▶ **Read Proverbs 30:18–19. Why do guys and girls like each other?**

The girls used to run from the boys. Now they chase them. Guys were afraid of girl germs. Now they want to get sick. True, some girls are still bored by boys and some guys still use girls as booger targets. That's okay. Sooner or later a trickle of curiosity about the opposite sex turns into a flood of fascination.

How are you going to handle that?

Love is easy to appreciate but hard to understand. It's like a restaurant that everyone agrees has great food, but where everyone picks a different favorite dish. Guys and girls are attracted to each other in baffling ways, like an eagle floating through the sky, a legless snake slithering across a rock, or a ship navigating the sea.

You never totally figure it out.

But it's time to start trying. You'll drown if you don't know that God has definite plans for how He wants you to get along with the opposite sex.

God isn't bashful. The Bible is blunt. And the parts of the Bible that talk about how girls and guys should get along weren't scribbled in by monks stuck at the monastery without a date. They were composed by the One who comprehends love best (1 John 4:7–8).

———————

There are four things that are too mysterious for me to understand: an eagle flying in the sky, a snake moving on a rock, a ship finding its way over the sea, and a man and a woman falling in love.

PROVERBS 30:18–19, GNB

14

Teased at the Table

"Josh and Cassie sitting in a tree, K-I-S-S-I-N-G. . . ." sasses Jenni across the supper table. "I saw them holding hands at the park."

"Dad, make her stop," Cassandra begs. "I said it nice. I didn't say 'Shut up!' "

"What's this?" her mother smirks as she pulls out a crumpled note. "I have a little evidence I found in the pocket of Cassie's jeans. It says here 'I love you, Josh.' With a big heart at the bottom. It sounds like *real* love to me."

Does she think this is cute? Cassandra wants to crawl under the table—and out the door and into the street and under a truck. *Does she think she's funny?*

Cassandra can't say what she feels: *I'm not a third-grader, Mom. Don't make fun of me. Josh is nice. I like him.*

She can predict her mom's response. "Sure you do, dear. That's so sweet."

☑ **Read 1 Corinthians 13:4–7. What is love actually like?**

You like someone. You decide to go together. You hold hands to show you belong to each other. You share a locker. At school you write notes and at home you hog the phone. People expect you to hang on each other.

That makes you uncomfortable. Some tell you to search for each other's tonsils with your tongues. You don't want to.

So what is love? How do you show it? How do you accept it?

Love is partly feelings. But a relationship won't last on tingles.

Love is partly physical. But most of that is out-of-bounds until you're married.

Real love is more than either of those. *Real love is a commitment in attitudes and actions to always do the best you can for another person.*

Still, it's harder to say what love *is* than what it looks like. People who love each other learn to be patient and kind. They avoid envy or boasting. They teach each other how to consider the other's feelings and to seek the other's best. They work to be slow to anger and to forget the wrongs they suffer. People in real love obey God. They protect, trust, and stick by each other.

Sound grown-up? Not exactly. It's the way all people should always act. And it's something you can practice now (Galatians 5:22–23).

Love is patient, love is kind. . . . It always protects, always trusts, always hopes, always perseveres.

1 CORINTHIANS 13:4, 7

15

What Does God Know About Bagging a Boy?

Eddie tried hard to get noticed by girls.

His rough-and-smelly stage peaked in seventh grade. That's when he slugged girls he liked. Or he tickled. If she giggled even a bit—how could she help it?— he thought, *She loves it! She loves me!* And when nothing else worked, body noises got him attention.

In eighth grade he progressed to arm wrestling, but no girl wanted to hold his hand. So he upped his sophistication. He quoted geometric proofs and chemical equations and obscure dates from Roman history. The girls thought he was dumb.

In ninth grade he got cool. He showered in his dad's cologne, undid the top three buttons on his shirt, slung a gold chain around his neck and said "Hey baby" a lot.

He smelled better but he was just as obnoxious.

☑ **Read Proverbs 3:1–4. How can you get noticed by the opposite sex?**

Your brain won't overheat coming up with *bad* ways to get attention:

If you're a guy: Challenge a girl to a belching contest. Ask a girl if she wanted her makeup to look like that or if a dog licked her. Spit watermelon seeds in a girl's ears. Mess up her bangs. Tell a dirty joke. Walk around with your neck muscles set at maximum flex.

Or if you're a girl: Get mad at a guy you like and make him guess why. Wear a skirt so tight you have to hop. Send messages through friends. Dye your hair a different color each week. Live to sit on boys' laps. Swipe a guy's hat and hide it forever. Tell a guy you want to be "just friends" and then never speak to him again.

What's the alternative?

You might doubt God knows how to bag a boy or get a girl. So you worry: *If I do what's right I'll be a nerd. If I'm nice they won't notice me. If I act like myself people won't like me. If I tell them I'm a Christian they'll think I'm weird.* And what does God say to try? Follow His commands and act loving and reliable toward everyone—which would make you secure, confident, loyal, and kind. Sounds awful, doesn't it?

Actually, it sounds like someone *you* would want to know.

Others will too.

Let love and faithfulness never leave you. . . . Then you will win favor and a good name in the sight of God and man.

PROVERBS 3:3A–4

16
Friends First

"We're not 'going together,'" Aaron protested. "We're friends."

In band Jessica was first chair and Aaron was second, a total humiliation to Aaron until she started helping him. He figured out she didn't care who was better. She liked that she didn't have to let him beat her and take first chair just because he was a guy.

Jessica had some explaining to do with her friends too. *He hasn't asked you to go anywhere? He hasn't bought you anything? Then why do you hang out with him?*

☑ **Read 2 Corinthians 6:14. What's the most important part of a guy-girl relationship?**

A guy-girl relationship is a great place to be—as long as you're not in a jail cell.

You're a prisoner to love: You worry about what you say, what you wear, how you look. If you talk to another guy or girl your cellmate goes nuclear. When you get labeled "boyfriend" or "girlfriend" you're best pals with some people and instant enemy to others. And a guy-girl relationship feels like prison for another reason: When your sentence is up you're out. Your friendship usually ends.

Few people are worth that. When you look back you wish you had a long-term friendship instead of a short-term relationship. So before you lock yourself up and eat the key, take a step back, go slow, and be friends first.

If you work at being friends instead of "going together," what's left?

Talking. Learning to not blab what you hear. Sharing hobbies. Surviving school together. Figuring out how to get along with his or her parents. Watching each other's games and concerts and recitals. Being friends with lots of friends, not being locked up with just one. And most of all, you should be able to grow together as Christians (2 Timothy 2:22).

Friendship is the most important part of a guy-girl relationship. And Christ is the most important part of the most important part.

God says never to "yoke" yourself (which describes going together, dating, marriage, or even being best friends) with someone who isn't a Christian. You would be like animals clamped together that plow in different directions. As you try to follow Christ, where would they drag you?

Find a friend plowing toward Christ just as fast and hard as you.

Do not be yoked together with unbelievers. . . .

2 CORINTHIANS 6:14

17

Crawl Back Into the Swamp

As the guys' gym class sat waiting for their pull-up test, Mark congratulated himself.

What timing! This is perfect. Mark knew he could do more pull-ups than any other guy. The girls' gym class was testing only a few feet away. *Julie can see me. She's going to think I'm so cool.*

"Mark!" the gym teacher hollered. "You're next!"

Tadd, the class thug, boosted Mark up to the bar. "Hey, Markie-poo!" Tadd snorted. "Julie's watching. Make her proud."

Julie turned when she heard her name. Mark did a pull-up. Two pull-ups. Three. The guys began to chant. "FOUR! FIVE! SIX! SEVEN!"

Then Tadd yanked Mark's gym shorts.

Mark was finished.

Read Isaiah 62:1–5. Does God ever think you're a reject?

Guys don't usually dream of their wedding day. They certainly don't picture themselves dressed in white from veil to toe, hitch-stepping down an aisle to "Here Comes the Bride," their beauty inspiring *oohs* and *aahs* and dropped jaws.

Yet even if you're a guy, that picture of a beautiful

bride is one to hammer into your head. God cherishes you—girl or guy—as a groom cherishes his bride. No bride is ugly to her groom. No groom says, "Crawl back in the swamp and fix your face." No groom stands at the altar and offers to trade his bride for someone else in the congregation. God likes you—and loves you—when no one else does (Romans 5:8).

God's people—ancient Israel, called "Zion" and "Jerusalem" here—were labeled "lonely" and "unlovely" by their enemies. God renamed His people "the delightful one" and "my bride."

God promises that when you're mocked or dumped or rejected that you still reflect His blazing glory. You're "a royal diadem crown in the hand of your God." And He promises that one day everyone will see you the way He does.

———

For the Lord will take delight in you . . . as a bridegroom rejoices over his bride, so will your God rejoice over you.

ISAIAH 62:4B–5

18

Hunk and Hunkette Hunting

A voice echoed in Keri's head. *Shouldn't you be doing your homework?*

"I suppose," Keri replied. "This is so much more interesting."

What's more interesting than math?

"Cutting out pictures for my wall—you know, of hunks—musicians, actors. . . ."

Why?

"I'm showing how special they are. I'm admiring their God-given qualities."

What do you think of boys when all they care about is how girls look?

"They're so shallow. I'm not like them. I don't drool."

How do you suppose the guys in the picture feel about you staring at them?

"They like to be looked at. I want them. And they're all mine."

☞ **Read 1 Thessalonians 4:1–8. What does it mean to "learn to control your own body"?**

You don't run through a supermarket tasting all the soda and squeezing all the fruit. You don't open a box of cereal, take a bite, and spill the rest on the floor.

Anyone knows that isn't the proper way to shop.

You don't taste, take, or wreck what doesn't belong to you. The Thessalonians, though, thought that when it came to sex they could ransack the supermarket, try before they buy, taste-test sexual love before marriage (called "fornication") or outside of marriage ("adultery").

Paul told them to control themselves. A footnote in many Bibles explains that Paul commanded them to "learn how to acquire a wife" in a way that pleases God. Anything less hurts not only the couple who disobeys God, but their future spouses. (That's what Paul means about "wronging a brother.")

To hunt for a hunk or hunkette in a holy and honorable way means you don't treat guys or girls as objects (Job 31:1). You speak with respect about them (Ephesians 5:3–4). And you back off when guys want to grab and girls want to hold.

You probably don't even realize you're shopping for a husband or a wife. But you're growing up—which means you've been flung into the supermarket.

It's a long time until checkout. Be careful how you handle the merchandise.

It is God's will . . . that you should avoid sexual immorality; that each of you should learn to control his own body [or, "learn to acquire a wife"] in a way that is holy and honorable. . . .

1 THESSALONIANS 4:3–4

19

Hotter Than a Nuclear-Powered Toaster

The sweetie you met on the second day of summer camp makes you sweat. You hold hands at the campfire, and as the fire crackles you sneak an arm around each other. You decide you want to burn lips at the basketball court, the camp's after-dark spot.

You want your first real kiss. Really bad. Your new friend hesitates, then says no.

What do you do? Multiple choice: (a) Kidnap the nearest available person of the opposite sex and bound to the basketball court; (b) Pretend that kissing bores you; (c) Hang out in the craft shop and make yourself a friendship bracelet; or (d) Spit at the feet of the person who rejected you.

📬 **Read Hebrews 13:4. God made sex great. How great?**

If you rate human experience from zero to ten, taking a bath with your hair dryer scores a definite zero—painful, scorching, and deadly. God intends sex to be *waaaaay* at the other end of the scale. But sex is only that great for those who wait.

To "honor the marriage bed" means to keep sexual intercourse—and the intense physical affection that precedes it—for marriage. Sex is God's wedding present to a man and a woman who seal their love through a public promise to stay together for life.

God's gift is hotter than a nuclear-powered toaster.

You don't want to power up now. Kissing starts a chain reaction God designed to end in an awesome explosion. If you feed fuel to the reactor *now*—in your thoughts, by what you watch and look at and listen to, by heated kissing, by the goals you set—you'll start a meltdown that sooner or later you won't stop.

The fire and fallout from breaking God's command are deadly. You worry about *conception*—creating a baby. Why gamble your future? You risk *infection*. Why risk death? You face *rejection*, when the relationship ends. Why torment yourself? And you won't escape *detection*. Why strain your most important relationship— your friendship with God?

So what's your choice? Another option: (e) Ask yourself some questions: Why do you want to get to the basketball court? Whose rules are you trying to play by?

Don't try so hard for your first kiss. Put your energy into waiting for the best.

Marriage should be honored by all, and the marriage bed kept pure, for God will judge the adulterer and all the sexually immoral.

HEBREWS 13:4

20
Dental Floss

Stephanie dashes from the changing house to a boulder along the beach—one not quite big enough to hide behind. It's just like her new swimsuit—not quite big enough to hide behind.

Stephanie thinks: *I can't believe I bought this. But it's too late now.*

The guys think: *Come on out, Steph! We think your swimsuit is great.*

The girls think: *She's so cheap. Why does she get all the attention? I wonder if I should get one of those.*

> **Read 1 Timothy 2:9–10. Why be modest?**

When you were little your parents taught you not to let people touch your "private parts." Big news: Your private parts are still private. You're the proud owner of a God-designed, almost-grown-up body.

Your goal is *not* to give away as much as you can (Proverbs 5:15–23).

Girls: When Paul wrote that women should "dress modestly," he wasn't picking on you. He knew that people—*especially* guys—are tempted by what they see. When you choose swimwear spun from a spool of dental floss you might as well mail the guys invitations to your birthday suit. To dress every day with "decency" and "propriety" you don't have to wear a bag. But you don't want to brag. Whenever you bait boys with your outward appearance you're asking them to see less than the real you.

Guys: That's NO excuse for you to grab with your eyes or your hands what isn't yours. When you start to want what you can't have, stare somewhere else (Matthew 5:27–30): Turn off the TV. Toss the magazine. Hang up the phone. Run away. Beg your girlfriend to cover up or find yourself a new girlfriend. Shut down the software.

Back to both of you: When you buy a present for a friend, you don't wrap it up and then kick it down the street or hurl it around a crowd. You would never hand a friend a torn and dirty gift. And a half-unwrapped present spoils the surprise.

You're the gift. Your spouse is the recipient. Take care of the present.

––––––––––––

I also want women to dress modestly, with decency and propriety. . . .

1 TIMOTHY 2:9

21
Tale of an Idiot

So-called scientists in white coats brief you before the experiment. "We're testing a new brand of stay-fresh sandwich bags," they inform you. "We've constructed a bag big enough for you to crawl into. We'll zip you inside, place you in a cage with a person-eating tiger, and watch what happens. Rest assured, nothing will happen. You'll be perfectly safe. Our new bag is totally airtight, so the tiger won't catch a whiff of you. And tigers won't eat what tigers can't smell."

"Any questions?" they ask.

Just one.

Are you that stupid? Would you trust your life to a sandwich bag?

▶ **Read Romans 16:17–20. What did Paul warn the Romans to watch out for?**

Your TV tells you to trust your life to a condom. Ads, friends, media—even some doctors, teachers, pastors, and parents—advise you to accept less than God's best.

They're like the people Paul warned the Romans against. They don't want what's best for *you*. They want to drag you into their disobedience, into following evil appetites instead of God, who is totally wise (Psalm 139:1–12) and totally loving (Psalm 145:17–18).

Paul says to flee from people figuring on feeding you to a tiger. But sometimes you don't even know you're being caged. No one ever bluntly told you how to tell good from evil.

Remember God's best? God made sex to be shared by a husband and wife, in order to be physically and emotionally united (Genesis 2:22–24).

Run away from the rest: Sex isn't for people not married to each other. Sex isn't a party game. Sex isn't a dare, or a contest to get as much as you can. Sexual contact is never for people of the same sex. The sex God invented isn't selfish, hurtful, violent, or controlling. Sex isn't something adults or teens do to children. Sex isn't a spectator sport for the screen or a magazine.

God's kind of sex is never dirty. It's private, but never something you have to keep secret or be embarrassed to talk about with an adult you trust.

Don't be stupid. Don't let anyone toss you to a tiger.

For such people are not serving our Lord Christ, but their own appetites. By smooth talk and flattery they deceive the minds of naive people.

Romans 16:18

22

This Means War

"Where are you and Brenda going after the game?" Tim's mom asked.

"I don't know," Tim shrugged. "We'll figure that out later."

Tim's parents looked at each other. *Say something,* they both silently said to each other.

"Are you planning to go out with anyone else?" Tim's dad tried to sound calm.

"I don't know yet."

"We don't think it's a good idea to leave your evening unplanned. We need to know where to find you," Tim's dad reasoned. "Why don't you call her now and ask what she wants to do?"

☛ Read James 4:7–10. Why do you need to plan, to decide ahead of time?

When you shoot rapids you don't shut your eyes, pull in your paddle, and trust your raft to go where it should. You declare war on the river. You jam your paddle into the water, pull and push, and work as a team with other rafters. Only then do you avoid getting knocked around, hung up, flipped out, or pulled under.

When parents ask your plans—with friends or with

a date—they aren't prying into your privacy. They need to know you'll be okay. More than that, they want *you* to know where you're going. They don't want you to drift wherever currents drag you.

James says to make the same decision about the whole of life. You have to *choose* not to drift, and to fight to stay upright. And you need to decide while the river is calm, before hormones swamp you and peers push and spin your raft.

When you "submit to God" you give Him your will. You say, "God, I want what *you* want." You declare that you're done drifting: You reject sin and get rid of "double-mindedness," halfhearted paddling. When you begin to understand the deadly dangers of sin you "grieve," "mourn," and "wail" for what you've done wrong. Powerful feelings.

But the end is clear: God will lift you free and set you paddling straight.

Growing up is one of the wildest rivers you'll ever run. God wants you to decide *now* to follow Him completely, and specifically, to stay pure sexually. You can write yourself a reminder of what you decide at the bottom of this page. Date it. Sign it. Celebrate it. And stick with it.

If you don't decide, then you've chosen to drift. And maybe drown.

———————

Submit yourselves, then, to God.

JAMES 4:7A

23

Their Pain, Your Gain

"You're going to do *what*? Why?"

"I don't know. I've wanted to for a while," your friend explains. "I'm curious. I'll do it once and I'll know."

"Don't you think it's wrong?"

"I don't think God would let me get hurt. He wants me to fit in, doesn't He? My friends keep saying I can't say what they're doing is wrong if I've never tried it myself."

How do I answer that one? Maybe she's right.

"Besides, I know my mom did when she was my age. She's always saying it was wrong. That's easy for her to say. She had her fun. She wants to spoil mine."

📭 **Read 1 Corinthians 10:1–14. How can you avoid making stupid mistakes?**

A friend climbs into a car and slams his hand in the door. He could assume one bash was an accident. He could call two bashes a coincidence. But after three bashes even the most thickheaded person should ponder what he's doing wrong.

Question: After watching your friend's mishaps, how many times would you have to crush your own hand in the car door before you would be careful?

The people of Israel had awesome experiences of God. He saved them from slavery in Egypt and led them to freedom in a cloud and pillar of fire. He gave them Moses' leadership and fed them with bread from heaven. Yet they turned away from what they knew. They chased evil instead of God, making fake gods (Exodus 32:1–6), sinning sexually (Numbers 25:1–9), and grumbling against God (Numbers 21:4–6).

You don't have to try sin to know that it's wrong and that sooner or later it hurts—whether it's doing drugs, drinking, going to an out-of-control concert, watching an R-rated movie, or sneaking out of the house. You can believe the Bible and your parents and other Christians when they say sin isn't the fun it's cracked up to be.

Experience is a great teacher—especially someone else's rotten experience. You're smart to learn from your own mistakes. But you're brilliant to learn from others' blunders. Their pain, your gain.

These things happened to them as examples and were written down as warnings for us. . . .

1 CORINTHIANS 10:11a

24

What You Want Is What You Get

Derek waves to his parents as they drive off. "See you later! Have fun!"

He knows *he'll* have fun. As Derek shuts the front door he wonders why his parents said not to have anyone over. *What are they worried about? Don't they trust me?*

A few minutes later the half dozen friends he invited arrive—followed a few minutes later by a half dozen he didn't invite. A guy Derek barely recognizes carries in a case of beer and asks directions to the fridge. A girl passes around a flask.

Things get loud. Things start to fall off walls.

Derek runs to the bathroom and locks himself in. *What to do? Call the cops on my own party?* Don't bother. The neighbors have already made the call. Red and blue lights flash in the driveway. Derek hears a knock at the front door and a scramble at the back. The officers are nice enough, but they promise to come back and chat with Derek's parents.

As Derek shuts the door he wonders if maybe his parents had a point.

📖 **Read Psalm 119:30–32. Does obeying God ever get easy?**

If you listen to your parents solely because they can ground you for life, then you'll always struggle with obeying. You'll think your parents' rules are prehistoric. You'll concentrate hard on how to bust boundaries—not how to keep them.

You'll only eagerly chase God's best when you trust Him above anything else. That doesn't happen all at once, but *how* it happens isn't hard to understand:

You stand. "Choose the way of truth" (verse 30). You tell God you want Him and His way. You read the Bible to remind yourself what God has done for you (Romans 10:17).

You walk. "Hold fast to God's statutes" (verse 31). You obey—even though you worry that you'll fall and grind your face in the dirt. But you don't. Over and over God shows that His ways work. He's kind and wise. Your trust grows.

So you run. Your feet find wings. You "run in the path of God's commands" (verse 32). Your heart is "set free" or "enlarged," which means "swollen with joy" (Isaiah 60:5), and "increased in understanding" (1 Kings 4:29).

You obey because you want to, not because you have to.

I run in the path of your commands, for you have set my heart free.

PSALM 119:32

PART 3

PLAYIN' SMART

25
First Things First

"Anyone else do their homework?" Silence.

Mike's cool, Nicole thought. Her Sunday school teacher never blew up at the class, even though no one except two nerds in the front row ever handed in homework.

Nicole shyly held up her paper. "Mine's done." She slumped in her seat. *I am not a nerd,* she reassured herself. *Then again, maybe I am turning into a nerd. Or maybe the nerds aren't so nerdy.* All Nicole knew for sure was that she felt better when she read her Bible and tried to talk to God like Mike talked about in class.

Anita grilled her after class. "I can't believe you actually did the homework. What's wrong with you? Don't you have anything better to do?"

"I don't know. I've done the last few. I might as well turn them in."

Then it occurred to Nicole that maybe she wasn't the one with a problem. "Don't *you* ever think about God?" she asked Anita. "Doesn't this stuff matter to you?"

✔ **Read Luke 10:38–42. What does Jesus say you need more than anything else?**

You've seen the symptoms of terminal adulthood: Sleepy reflexes. Saggy clothes. Not to mention petrification—brains as dense as rock. Or putrefaction—rotting attitudes.

The middle part of *adult*, you note, is *dull*. No one wants that.

But Mary—along with a bunch of other men and women in the Bible—shows how to mature without getting moldy. Mary's kind of stillness won't mellow you prematurely.

It's hard to talk to a friend when you're sprinting. You can't converse while blasting a hill on a mountain bike. If you want to get to know a friend there's no substitute for slowing down—talking over a gooey pizza or lounging next to a glassy lake or flopping on your bed with the phone.

Jesus wants you to be like Mary, to slow down and spend time with Him. By reading His word—the Bible—you "sit at his feet" and hear *from* Him. By praying—by telling Him what you think and feel, what you like about Him, asking for His help—you can talk *to* Him.

Of everything you can choose to do in a day it's the first thing you really need.

And it's one kind of sitting still that doesn't mean you're dull.

She had a sister called Mary, who sat at the Lord's feet listening to what he said.

LUKE 10:39

26

Perseverance Precedes the Presidency

"The printouts I'll distribute in a few minutes," your guidance counselor drones, "suggest a number of occupations appropriate for you, based on your individual academic achievement, aptitude test scores, and personality profiles. . . ."

Just show us the sheets. We know what they are. For weeks you had taken tests meant to spark your interest in a career. Your test results, you're sure, will disclose your multitudinous gifts and career choices. You already know what you want to be: *Pro tennis player. CIA special agent. Movie producer. Jet pilot. Oceanographer.*

"Don't look at your sheets," your counselor cautions, "until I say."

You peek. Only two choices.

That's okay. It's probably President of the United States and Treasury Secretary.

Look again.

Burger flipper. French fry dipper.

📭 **Read 2 Corinthians 11:23–33. What price did Paul pay to accomplish his goals?**

Paul aimed for two things in life: to know Christ (Philippians 3:7–11) and to tell the world about Him (2

Corinthians 5:18–20). When God appointed Paul a preacher he considered it such a privilege that even shipwrecks and whippings didn't make him quit. He took a beating and rebounded off the ropes.

Goals are easier to dream about than to accomplish.

Paul knew that actions—what you do right now—matter more than boasting about what you'll be. You won't become a rocket scientist if you never shoot higher than C minus. You won't play in the symphony if you don't rehearse for real. You won't ever practice medicine if you don't practice caring about people now.

James wrote that when you have faith—when you trust God to lead your life—that you will "persevere," trample over, around, or through obstacles. You rely on God to help you dig into your dream and then finish what you start.

Perseverance isn't pain without a purpose. It makes you "mature," "complete," and "lacking nothing" (James 1:2–4). So you can reach your dreams for real.

I have worked much harder. . . .

2 Corinthians 11:23

27

Hold the Heimlich Maneuver

"What was her question today?"

"She asked how we know that God made the world and that we didn't evolve."

"Maybe that's her problem. She's an ape."

"She thinks too hard. We're just supposed to accept stuff. Aren't we?"

"All this started when her grandma died. She asked Pastor Lee if heaven was real and he gave her this big huge lecture. She feels really bad."

"Did you see Mr. Swenseid's face when she asked if Jesus really did a miracle to feed all those people? He stopped breathing. I swore he had a heart attack. That's one thing I don't like. I don't like it when they act like we're little and don't have questions."

▶ **Read John 1:43–51. Is it bad to ask questions about your faith?**

You can't swallow food whole. Either the gastric guards in your esophagus forcibly expel the intruder or your stomach grinds to a halt when the goo in your gut asks who let the solids in. Or you choke and die.

God doesn't expect you to swallow truth whole. He wants you to chew.

Nathanael was skeptical. He questioned whether Jesus was who Philip claimed He was, God's Son come to save the world.

But Nathanael also accepted Philip's invitation to come and see. That's different from refusing to believe anything no matter what the evidence. That's different from acting too cool for Sunday school—writing off Bible study or youth group or confirmation class without even trying to understand your faith.

Jesus saw him under the fig tree—a customary spot for studying Scripture. Nathanael knew where to look for answers. He was like the Bereans (Acts 17:11), who heard the message Paul preached about Christ "with great eagerness and examined the Scriptures every day to see if what Paul said was true."

Nathanael wasn't crabby. He wasn't making excuses. He loved truth enough to ask questions, chew on the answers, and live (2 Thessalonians 2:10). Being mature doesn't mean you know everything. It means you know the One who does.

When Jesus saw Nathanael approaching, he said of him, "Here is a true Israelite, in whom there is nothing false."

JOHN 1:47

28

Power Steering

Megan cracked a wicked smile when her aunt and uncle and cousins pulled into the driveway. They lived in a state where it never snowed. Last summer her cousins nearly drowned her in the ocean. They called her a hick.

Now it was winter. And they were on her turf.

Megan tossed them some ice skates and herded them to a frozen pond out back. It was time to race.

Race? They couldn't stand up. Cold air burned their lungs. Then when their toes got cold and they wanted to go inside, Megan swooped in for the kill. She buzzed circles around them. They sprawled. She hipchecked. They smacked ice.

On the way inside she told them she had one more cool thing to try—licking a flagpole. "Helffffph!" they yelled, their tongues frozen to the pole.

"You deserve that," Megan screamed as she went in to warm up. "I hate you!"

📝 **Read Judges 16:23–30. How can you get good at something without getting snotty?**

Samson's conceit about his strength was the only thing bigger than his muscles (Judges 11–15). So when he let his Philistine girlfriend sweet-talk him into revealing the secret of his might, God allowed his enemies to grab him, gouge out his eyes, and toss him in prison to grind wheat like a mule (Judges 16:21).

Samson became powerful again only when he was tamed—when he remembered that because his strength came *from* God it should be used *for* God. Instead of using his strength for himself alone, he handed the Philistines—a nation at war with Israel—a rather crushing defeat.

When you're smart or skilled you have a choice: Gently clue people in on what you know, or smear brains in their faces. When you're strong you can use your strength to help people, or to break their thumbs. And when you're funny you choose between cheering people up, or pounding them down.

Remember that the strongest people are the ones who don't have to prove their strength.

Then Samson prayed to the Lord, "O Sovereign Lord, remember me. O God, please strengthen me just once more. . . ."

JUDGES 16:28

29

He Ain't Ugly—
He's My Cousin

"Isn't that exciting?" your mom had suddenly asked. Your life flashed before your eyes. There wasn't much to see. With your cousin switching to your school, life was over.

Henry looked like a giant prehistoric beaver you once saw at a natural science museum, minus the tail—beady eyes and teeth that would make a mamma beaver proud, topped by glasses like soda-bottle bottoms.

You thought about introducing him to a friend whose dad was a plastic surgeon, but instead you faked sick and stayed home for the first three days he was at school. Then it hit you. *We have different last names. No one will ever know.*

Your solution worked until someone swiped his glasses. He was pitiful, with his teeth chattering as he whimpered.

"Give them back. NOW!" you hear yourself say.

Why do you care? You tell them he's your cousin. Life is definitely done.

▶ **Read Ruth 1:1–6. Why was Ruth loyal to her mother-in-law?**

Some obligations were thrust on Ruth. While her husband lived she had a duty to her mother-in-law,

Naomi. But she *chose* other obligations. She stuck with Naomi—someone who had been good to her. She decided to follow God and to join a new nation.

You're "loyal" when you meet the obligations you should—to God (1 Chronicles 29:17–18), family (Exodus 20:12), country (Romans 13:1), people who have helped you (Luke 17:12–16), other believers (Galatians 6:10), and people in need (Luke 10:29–37).

And it's a mistake to misplace loyalty—to give it to material things (Matthew 6:24), or to people who hurt you (2 Corinthians 11:19–20). Being loyal doesn't mean you keep a friend's suicide note a secret, or shield a friend who did wrong (Ephesians 5:11). Being loyal sometimes means you hurt a friend to help him.

So what deserves your loyalty—and how much—and why? Think it through: (*a*) Your bratty sister; (*b*) Your homely next-door neighbor who's been your best friend since kindergarten; (*c*) A popular peer who brushes you off like dirt; (*d*) Your dad when he dresses dumb; (*e*) Your favorite football team; or (*f*) Your best pair of hightops.

Don't die for something dumb. But don't hide when something important deserves your help.

But Ruth replied, "Don't urge me to leave you or to turn back from you. Where you go I will go, and where you stay I will stay. Your people will be my people and your God my God."

Ruth 1:16

30
The Price Is Right

"This one. Definitely the coolest." Paul's friends each grabbed a sweatshirt blazoned with their school's logo and headed to the cashier to pay.

"Aren't you going to buy one?" Chris asked. "We're all getting them."

"Nope. Maybe later."

"How come you never have money?" Chris nosed.

Steve sneered. "He doesn't make any money. He volunteers as a handiwipe at the nursing home. He changes old people's diapers."

"I don't change diapers," Paul fought back. "So what if I did? My job's more important than mowing lawns to make money for a sweatshirt."

"You don't get paid?" Chris was shocked. "That's stupid. Why work?"

▶ Read Luke 21:1–4. How do you figure the value of a gift?

Your dog won't know the difference if you stuff yourself silly *before* you flip a few measly scraps under the table.

But that's no way to treat people. Jesus says that when you love people you don't just give leftovers. Even though the gift the widow gave was tiny, Jesus said it was better than the bags of money the rich gave. She offered all she had.

Real gifts cost you something.

Your gift might be to help little kids at church, volunteer at a latch-key program, or tutor during free time at school. Giving unselfishly might cost you *time*.

You could choose to contribute monthly to provide a child with school, food, shelter, and clean water. Or you can give to projects where you live. Being a giver often costs *money*.

And Jesus says to target people who can never pay you back (Luke 14:12–14), to reach beyond your crowd of friends to the poor, strange, sick, or trapped (Matthew 25:34–36). You might not like those people. They might not like you. They probably aren't the people you normally hang out with. So giving a real gift can cost you *popularity*.

Loving unselfishly sometimes costs you even more. It can cost you everything—as it did the widow. But that's the kind of gift Jesus gave to you (1 John 3:16).

———————

"I tell you the truth," he said, "this poor widow has put in more than all the others. All these people gave their gifts out of their wealth; but she out of her poverty put in all she had to live on."

LUKE 21:3–4

31

Honest to God

"It's not fair!" Sandy was ticked. "He failed half of us." When she saw Mr. Denter's office empty and unlocked before school, she rampaged. Sandy cleared the top of his desk and yanked the desk drawers onto the floor.

Then her friend Kendra joined in by feeding a jelly sandwich to a VCR stored behind Mr. Denter's desk.

Sandy froze. "Kendra! What are you doing?"

"They'll never figure out we did it. They'll think it was the guys from class."

That day Sandy told Mr. Denter she needed to talk after class. "I messed up your desk," she confessed. "I'll help you pick stuff up, and then I'll go see the principal."

"You're going to be a little hungry at lunch today, aren't you?" he prodded.

"I didn't do that!" Sandy argued. "Honest!"

"You'll have to explain that at the office, Sandy. I'm not sure I believe you."

> Read Psalm 51:1–12. When is it right to admit that you're wrong?

David wrote Psalm 51 after he had an affair with Bathsheba and ordered her husband killed so he could take her as his wife. That's big sin. But to God there's not much difference between David's sin and ours. All sin builds a wall between us and God.

Sin hurts everyone, but God more than anyone. He's the "you" in "against you, you only have I sinned." David could make no excuses or bargains with God, who is the ultimate judge of right and wrong. David's only hope was to come clean and plead for mercy.

David wanted God to forget his "transgressions," to stop being angry with him, and to fix their friendship. God answers that request. He promises to forgive those who are truthful with Him about what they've done wrong (1 John 1:8–9).

And David knew it would be dishonest to grab God's forgiveness, then go and sin more. So he asked God to help him be happy doing what God required. That's another request God promises to grant to those who ask (Jeremiah 31:33–34).

Experiencing forgiveness and a faithful heart begins when you're truthful to God and yourself. Little kids can pretend they're things they're not—a pirate, a princess, a pro athlete. But to grow up you need to see yourself as you are. No more, no less. Honest.

––––––––––––––

Against you, you only, have I sinned and done what is evil in your sight, so that you are proved right when you speak and justified when you judge.

PSALM 51:4

32

All Tied Up and Somewhere Better to Go

Courtney sat on the curb outside the gym, crying. "I don't want them to see me like this. I'm so sick of them.

"Shawna started it. She said I was ugly and laughed at me and talked behind my back, even though she said I was her best friend.

"She said I tried to steal her boyfriend from her. He and I had three classes together. I just talked to him. That's not illegal, is it? I'm not a flirt. She is.

"And then three weeks ago she said *really* bad stuff about me—stuff I wouldn't say about anyone." Courtney started to cry again. "When I tried to defend myself it was even worse. It's been *three weeks* since any of my friends have talked to me. They all hate me now.

"And I hate *her*."

Read 1 Peter 2:19–23. Why should you forgive people who hurt you?

You trash your sister's boombox and she makes you buy a new one. You skip practice and get benched. You come tardy to school and get detention.

You got punished. You deserved it. Big deal. Take your lumps.

But you don't earn every bad thing that hits you—

like when people lie about you, mock your beliefs, blame you for something you didn't do, or question your motives or friendship. Or when they rip you off or broadcast your smallest mistake.

Jesus said believers should "turn the other cheek" (Matthew 5:39). That doesn't mean you let people slap you up. Jesus said to confront people who pain you, and to avoid them if they don't change (Matthew 18:15–17).

Even if you can change a bad situation, your hurts don't go away if you keep hating. Your enemies will still hit your heart, and hating them only ropes and gags you. You won't feel free until you forgive.

Jesus forgave by praying for the people who hurt Him (Luke 23:34). Then He refused to plot revenge or to toss back insults. He let God defend Him.

By forgiving His enemies Jesus wrestled free from them.

Forgiveness gets you off the curb and back into life.

————————

When they hurled their insults at him, he did not retaliate. . . . Instead, he entrusted himself to him who judges justly.

1 PETER 2:23

33

Don't Go Solo

As his home for the next seventy-two hours Bob picked a strip of land jutting into a backwoods lake. If he could live with nothing more than a sleeping bag—constructing his own shelter, starting his own fire, snaring his own food—he would pass his survival skills test.

Halfway through Bob's second day a swarm of biting black flies attacked him. He almost cried. He ducked inside his sleeping bag for protection—head and all—but he baked like a pig in a blanket. So he crawled back out to fight flies.

Later that night when Bob was back in the bag wishing he had found more to eat, a storm blew up and the wind nearly rolled him off the point. Bob yelled. He ran through the rain to rocks not far away. As he slid into a crevice he knew he had broken the rules for the solo. He had left his solo site. He was safe. But he felt as if he had failed.

📝 **Read Luke 1:26–38. Where did Mary hide when she felt overwhelmed?**

Life isn't a cushy motorhome campout. You might get sick. Or parents split. A friend moves. You move. You fight with a friend and you might as well have moved. You bust your brain trying to learn at school. Or peers threaten to bust your head because you're too smart.

Maturity means knowing enough to run for cover when you know you can't make it alone.

When an angel knocked at Mary's door and said that God had an astounding plan for her life, Mary had a big question: *How can I have a son? I've never been with a man.* But her baby wouldn't be made the ordinary way. He would be formed by the Holy Spirit. And Jesus wouldn't be an ordinary baby. He was God's Son, Savior of the world.

People will still talk, Mary must have thought. *I'll be an outcast.* Even Joseph decided to break their engagement until God told him the plan (Matthew 1:19).

Mary saw in God's plans for her life both wonder and terror. But she knew where to run from the storm. She was tough—even though she was possibly barely a teenager—because she hid in the Rock (Isaiah 26:3–4). Mary knew whom to trust.

You won't earn a merit badge for trying to survive life solo. You've only failed if you don't hide in the Rock and end up getting blown away.

———

"I am the Lord's servant," Mary answered. "May it be to me as you have said. . . ."

LUKE 1:38

34

No Fear

Everyone called them "The Dwarfs," but not because they were short. The seven girls got their nickname when they started playing basketball together in elementary school. By the end of middle school they were best friends—and the core of the best team around, sure to power their small high school to a state title.

And the Dwarfs were Dwarfs because they *hi-ho-hi-ho*ed everywhere together—on or off court. They dressed, talked, and poofed their hair the same. Whoever they liked was popular. Whoever they disliked was scum.

The clump fell apart when two Dwarfs became Christians. "That isn't what Dwarfs do," the other five told Kelli and Elise. "We're not into God." That started a tough game of five-on-two. On the court the other girls pushed Kelli and Elise out of plays. Off the court they turned their backs and walked away.

Kelli and Elise didn't see any way to win that game.

✔ **Read Numbers 14:1–9. When the Israelites refused to enter the good land that God had promised them, how did Joshua and Caleb stand up to the crowd?**

When peers try to force you to follow their rules they usually don't toss you an exploding basketball. They don't press a gun to your head and shout, "Cheat! Steal! Cut people down! Slack off at school! Scream at your parents!"

They play mind games (Romans 12:2). They make you think your world will fall apart without them. And they don't *force* you to follow—you *choose* to do what they want because you believe two lies: (1) *Doing wrong to please them is more important than doing right to please yourself; and (2) Making them happy matters more than making God happy.* Peers get power over you because you give it to them.

The people of Israel said God was mean and His followers idiots. They feared that giants in the promised land would slaughter them. Joshua and Caleb struck back with truth—that the God of might would do them right. They refused to rebel against God. They refused to fear the crowd.

Because Joshua and Caleb dared to be different, God blessed them (Numbers 14:30). They turned out to be the real giants.

Only do not rebel against the LORD. *And do not be afraid of the people of the land, because we will swallow them up. Their protection is gone, but the* LORD *is with us. . . .*

NUMBERS 14:9

35

Buena Contesta

You hate that Papa Smurf know-it-all look your older brother gets on his face when he's serious.

"I'm worried about you," he says as he sits you down on the couch. "I've done some dumb stuff I don't want you to do."

You wonder what stupid things he did to make him feel the need to straighten you out. *We knew all along that you were dumb. What's your point?*

"Some of those kids you're hanging around are trouble," he advises. You squirm. He's right. Then your brother gets an odd look. He starts to cry. That's never happened before. "I know I've treated you like a dirtball," he apologizes. "But I really care about you. You need to be smart. I hope you'll listen to what I say."

You stare at him wiping his eyes and wonder if that's what it's like to grow up.

📩 **Read 1 Kings 3:5–15. Why did Solomon ask God to make him wise?**

You thought God was supposed to tell *you* what to do. But there He is in a dream, asking what you want Him to give you. It's phenomenal cosmic power at your fingertips.

What would you ask for? The ability to run a hundred yards in 3.6 seconds? To captain the starship Enterprise? Maybe for your worst enemy to die in a sudden freak accident? How about sole ownership of Microsoft?

Think bigger.

Wishing for wisdom would be like wishing for more wishes. Thinking the way God thinks tells you what to pursue and how to catch it. Wisdom makes every part of maturity—being close to God, steadfast, thoughtful, strong, loyal, unselfish, forgiving, honest, dependent on God, and free from peer fear—that much more grown-up.

Okay, okay. Wisdom is best. So who should you ask to help you get wise? Your friend's parents who, you've noted, aren't smart enough to ever say *no*? Nah. Your older sister or brother? Maybe. Maybe not. A friend? Won't work. You may know people as cool as you, but surely none as bright.

How about God? He's the one Being in the universe who knows everything.

Good answer.

"I will do what you have asked. I will give you a wise and discerning heart, so that there will never have been anyone like you, nor will there ever be."

1 KINGS 3:12

PART 4

STEERIN'
STRAIGHT

36

Wise Guy

Pen and narrow-ruled notebook at the ready, you lean forward in your seat and strain to appear as intelligent as the other students in your first college class. Your professor strolls in, easy to spot in his tweed jacket, gray hair and goatee. His accent informs everyone that he was born on the distant island of Academia.

As your professor explains his requirements for you to earn an *A*, *B*, or *C*, a guy with a pocket protector waves his hand wildly. "Is this going to be on the test?" he asks. The professor sneers at him, and students look down their noses. "Leave now," your professor warns the class, "if you're not planning on *working* to earn a *C*. You will work, or you won't pass."

You wince.

"You will succeed," he continues, "if you remember two things: *I* am here because I know more than you. *You* are here to benefit from my wisdom."

You cringe. Yet you know he's right.

Read Proverbs 1:1–7. Where do you go to get smart?

Life is a string of events in which others do for you what you can't do—and teach you what you don't know—until you grow capable yourself.

So admit it: Sometimes, in some situations, you're helpless and dumb.

Don't feel bad. So is everyone else. We all need what God wants to teach: "wisdom" (knowing how to live skillfully), "discipline" (training in obeying God), "discretion" (choosing rightly between two ideas or two actions), and "prudence" (thinking through actions before you do them). God's wisdom rescues you from being simple or immature so you know how to act well toward yourself and others.

The incredible part is that the all-knowing God never treats you like an idiot. He isn't a professor parading His vastly superior knowledge.

But *He can only teach you as much as you want to know.* You get smart only when you "fear God"—when you respectfully submit to His teaching because you know that you need Him to figure out life.

You'll always need to learn from the Father who knows best.

The proverbs of Solomon son of David, king of Israel
. . . for giving prudence to the simple, knowledge
and discretion to the young. . . .

PROVERBS 1:1, 4

37

Thugs 'Я' Us

"Here it is." Brenda flipped through the movie listings in the evening paper. "It's showing at 9:00. Let's go."

Terese moaned. "My parents said to be home at 9:30."

"So?" Linda practically told her parents when *they* should be home.

"Do the math, O brainy one," Terese shot back. "The movie is two hours long. I'd be a little late."

"Since when do you listen to your parents?" Linda inquired.

Brenda had an idea. "Can't you call your parents and tell them you'll be late?"

"They'll say no. We're leaving early in the morning for my grandparents to—"

Brenda cut her off. "We're going. You can go home if you want."

"You know what your problem is?" Linda asked. "You're not any fun."

✔ **Read Proverbs 1:10–19. How do you spot a thug?**

The thugs you know probably look nicer than the thieves in Proverbs. They dress like you. They talk like you. They live in your neighborhood and go to your school. They want the same stuff you do.

The thugs you know most likely don't lie in ambush to burglarize and butcher innocent pedestrians. But they still aim to rob others to enrich themselves—to look good, feel big, be popular, set the rules, and get what they want.

The thugs you know move in cliques and pick easy targets. Even without weapons they leave a trash trail—busted feelings, broken promises, stolen property, disappointed parents, wounded bodies, and stabbed hearts.

You know enough to run from tough hoods who whisper at you from alleys. It's the thugs nearby that you have to beware of—the ones who stop calling, stop saying "Hi!" in the hall, and stop being your friend when you don't join them.

And there's a thug inside you that you have to guard against. It's the part of you that wants to take by force or by stealth what isn't yours (James 4:1–2).

Thugs aren't always strangers on the street. Sometimes the thugs are us.

My son, if sinners entice you, do not give in to them.

Proverbs 1:10

38
What a Trip

Your social studies teacher was fresh from college, but she looked as if she'd found her bell-bottoms in a musty box in her dad's closet. You called her Moonmuffin.

A chia pet on Moonmuffin's desk daily blessed her tofu sandwich with fresh sprouts. Scattered around her desk were crystals she said kept her from getting sick.

You said they were pretty. She said they were powerful.

And when the class studied the Salem Witch Trials she offered to read palms and brought in a "white witch" to speak. "She's wonderful," Moonmuffin gushed. "She harnesses the power of nature to do good." *Yeah, right*, you thought. *She tries to harness the power of rabid dogs and bat fangs and killer sharks. This is our role model?*

The last you heard, Moonmuffin had been nailed by a truck while meditating against air pollution on a freeway overpass.

🏁 **Read Proverbs 1:20–33. What happens to people who refuse to get smart?**

You don't want to recognize yourself in this section of Proverbs. You don't want to be *simple*—dim-witted, too stupid to watch where you're going. You don't want to be a *mocker*—sharp-tongued, too proud to accept advice. And you definitely don't want to be *foolish*—stubborn, too headstrong to be corrected, apt to repeat your mistakes like a dog that chomps its own vomit (Proverbs 26:11).

The simple, mockers, and foolish have a few things in common. They like themselves just the way they are. They live as if God didn't exist. And catastrophe will liquidate them because they continually reject wisdom.

Not smart.

You won't straighten out every person in the world who rejects God. But it *is* your job to be ready and able to explain your faith—with gentleness and respect—to everyone who asks you to explain why you entrust your life to Christ (1 Peter 3:15).

And it's your job to not be duped when they try to sell you a different god—or no God—or rewritten rules of right and wrong. Understand what they say. But understand too where they go wrong. After all, you can be so open-minded that your brain falls out.

"For the waywardness of the simple will kill them, and the complacency of fools will destroy them; but whoever listens to me will live in safety and be at ease, without fear of harm."

PROVERBS 1:32–33

39

Dig It?

Phil had heard high school was so tough that he panicked his freshman and sophomore years. He studied hard. He pulled better grades than anyone expected.

So halfway through he decided to slack off.

At the end of one semester his counselor called him to his office. "At this rate you won't graduate on time," his counselor warned him. "You understand that, don't you? What are you going to do about it?"

Phil promised to work hard, but his promises got to be a joke. He goofed around in class and study halls and after school. *I'm just doing what my friends are doing*, he told himself.

Spring semester of his senior year he didn't have enough credits to graduate.

Oops.

📑 **Read Proverbs 2:1–11. Will you get smart if you just wait long enough?**

You didn't quite hear her. You thought she said there was gold buried in your backyard.

Your next question wouldn't be "Did you say something?" or "Were you talking to me?" or "Excuse me, I didn't quite catch that. Would you be so kind as to repeat what you said a moment ago?" You would say,

"Did you say GOLD? WHERE?"

And if you didn't understand the message the first time, you would scream for a clear answer. You would scoop, shovel, excavate, and detonate until you found gold.

That's "crying aloud for understanding" and "searching for wisdom as hidden treasure." It's not enough to want wisdom. You must search for it.

High school graduation doesn't just happen. You don't get smart without studying. And wisdom doesn't just drop in your lap.

Attaining wisdom is a far-off goal like graduating from high school. The wisdom you get from God by studying the Bible (2 Timothy 3:16–17) isn't something you always use right away. That makes it tempting to give up, to slacken your search. But the only way to get wise is to keep at it, to store up wisdom so you have it when you need it.

And no one will dig for you.

If you call out for insight and cry aloud for understanding . . . then you will understand the fear of the Lord and find the knowledge of God.

PROVERBS 2:3, 5

40

The Secret Service Comes to School

Why the President wanted to visit your school no one knew. But one day your principal announced he was coming. *The* President. Of the United States. And your principal launched a school-wide essay contest: "What I Want to Ask the President."

Whoever won the contest would get lunch with the President. You wanted to win bad—not so you could discuss the finer points of foreign policy but to chum with the big cheese. So you titled your entry "Why I Want to Yuck It Up With the Yo-Yo."

When you lost the contest you plotted ways to get the President's attention. Then bomb-sniffing dogs checked lockers and secret service agents toting burp guns under their suitcoats banged through ventilation ducts. You decided that sitting in the front row and playing "Hail to the Chief" on your armpit wasn't such a hot idea. You didn't want the President to target a nuclear missile on your locker or to snap a spy-satellite picture of you picking your nose when you thought no one was looking.

It's not good to mess with the President.

☑ **Read Proverbs 2:5. What is "the fear of the Lord"?**

God calls Christians closer to himself than you'll ever get to a President. He offers to be your friend (Revelation 3:20). Because Christ died for your sins you have a constant relationship with the God of the universe (Hebrews 10:19–22). That beats any invitation to the Oval Office.

But knowing God is more than just hanging with the head honcho.

To "fear God" doesn't exactly mean you're scared spitless. God is totally powerful. That might push you away in fear. Yet God is totally loving. His kindness pulls you toward Him. Put those together: You're drawn to God in awe and respect.

The book of Nahum illustrates how to think about God. There *are* reasons to dread Him. He's a "jealous and avenging God" (1:2) and "He will not leave the guilty unpunished" (1:3). But God is also "a refuge in times of trouble" (1:7). He "cares for those who trust in Him" (1:7).

You're a fool to put your hand in a fire. But you're a bigger fool not to come close and be warmed by its heat.

Then you will understand the fear of the LORD *and find the knowledge of God.*

PROVERBS 2:5

41

Nightmare

You shouldn't have watched the late news before you went to bed. You feel besieged: *Double murder-suicide. Flesh-eating streptococcus germs. Carjacking on the corner. Drugs in schoolyards. Satanists carving up animals in the country. Kidnappers crawling through windows. Nuclear materials lost in the former Soviet Union. Drug cartels flourishing in South America. Political dissidents oppressed in Asia. Bodies floating down rivers in Africa. Children starving everywhere.*

Solutions?

You could build an arsenal of megaplasma lasers and neutron grenades and hide under your bed.

Or you could be wise where you walk.

☑ **Read Proverbs 2:12–22. What dangers in life are worth worrying about?**

Humans have always faced obvious outside threats. From woolly mammoths to the risk of worldwide thermonuclear war, history hasn't been wholly wonderful.

Life has definitely been worse: The Plague. Crossing the Atlantic. Slavery. Child labor. The Holocaust.

But the world could surely be better. You want a long and happy life—emphasis on "long" and "happy."

You expect circumstances to improve as you age. But you worry that by the time you grow up there won't be anything left to enjoy.

Danger feels like it's on your doorstep. TV thrusts you into wars and murder investigations and drug busts, and it drops dying children on your family room floor. You see the world's problems but become blind to the dangers most likely to do *you* in.

You are the biggest threat to you. The biggest factor in foreseeing your future is how well *you* follow God's pattern for life. A nightstalker crawling in through your window is far less a real threat than *you* crawling out at night, losing your moral and spiritual footing, and falling off the roof.

Growing up won't get easier. Yet you don't grow to adulthood alone. Trusting in God makes you a well-watered tree that doesn't fear when heat comes (Jeremiah 17:8). And you band together with others to battle what you can't beat by yourself.

Then you'll live to help fix the problems out there.

Wisdom will save you from the ways of wicked men. . . .

PROVERBS 2:12

42

His Way the Highway

"Would you rather stay here or run in with me?" your dad asks.

"Here. Just leave me the keys."

As soon as Dad is out of sight you clamber into the driver's seat, move the mirrors, and tilt the wheel. Best of all, you find *your* station on the stereo. You settle back on your throne. It's a moment of paradise in the quickmart parking lot.

In two years, eight months, and eleven days you'll take revenge on the world for being held back in kindergarten: You'll get your driver's license a year before any of your friends. It's a long wait, but you need the time to convince your parents to dump the family roadster and procure a car more suitable to your style.

Driving is your dream.

So where are you going to go?

☑ **Read Proverbs 3:5–12. What does God promise when you travel His road?**

You've got transportation. What's your destination? You've got freedom. Where do you want to wind up?

Maybe you want to blast your car down curvy roads. That *would* be a blast—if you like to soar ditchward in a wingless vehicle.

God plans a kinder, gentler end for you if you know Him. You trust in the Lord with all your heart—unlike people who aren't sure what they want (James 4:8). You don't live solely by your own brains—you seek guidance from the Smartest One. The result? God powers you straight and fast.

Another way of looking at it: You know that compared to God you're not wise. You respect God's evaluation of good and evil. Once again—the result: It does your body and soul good.

God's way is straight, but not bumpless. God's discipline jars you awake and keeps your eyes on His road. But it's still smoother than ramping offroad.

You can choose to drive in the ditch.

But when you choose His way over your way you fly the highway.

Trust in the Lord with all your heart and lean not on your own understanding; in all your ways acknowledge him, and he will make your paths straight.

PROVERBS 3:5–6

43

Time Warped

Fast forward your life twenty-five years.

You stare at your home computer, reviewing your monthly family finances. It looked simpler when you were little and your parents sat down with a stack of bills and the checkbook at the kitchen table.

"Honey, I don't know how we can do this!" you vent. "The mortgage, the car payment, and Becky's orthodontist bill are due at the same time. We can either live in the street or go hungry. Which would you prefer?" For the next three hours the two of you discuss ways to increase income and cut expenses.

What's the moral of the story? That you should ride bikes, rent a tent, and throw back any children with crooked teeth?

Nope. It's that no one is going to pay your bills for you.

☑️ **Read Proverbs 6:6–11. Why work?**

You might want to cheat at your chores—to bill your parents for five hours labor cleaning the garage when you spent four hours of that time sucking soda. You'll bite the dust when you get a real boss on your back.

You might think you can take shortcuts on your schoolwork—and flip to the back of the book to find the right answer. You'll hit the fan when you take a test. Whenever you just get by you always get behind. The admissions office at Harvard won't ask how you did in eighth grade math. But they'll be able to guess. What you study now prepares you for high school, which fits you for even more serious stuff. If you waste away in middle school you'll be three years behind students who decided not to dangle on the edge of disaster.

When God gives you school, chores, or other jobs to do, learn to work *now* "with all your heart, as working for the Lord, not for men, since you know that you will receive an inheritance from the Lord as a reward. It is the Lord Christ you are serving" (Colossians 3:23–24).

You don't have to manage cars, kids, braces, bosses, bills, houses, or hassles for a while.

But you're in training.

Go to the ant, you sluggard; consider its ways and be wise! It has no commander, no overseer or ruler, yet it stores its provisions. . . .

PROVERBS 6:6–8A

44

Nick Meets Dawn

"I guess we're partners. My name is Dawn."

Duh. I know who you are. Did you know that every guy in the grade likes you?

"Hi. I'm Nick." Dawn didn't have the best reputation. Everyone said she drank a lot. Everyone knew her boyfriend sold drugs out of his locker. *But she's beautiful. That stuff can't be true.*

One day when they were working together Nick needed to get Dawn's attention. He tapped her arm. *Wowsy!* It was the softest thing he had ever felt!

When he showed her what he had finished she grabbed his hand. "I'd be failing if it weren't for you. Thanks. You're really nice." *Wowsy-woo-woo!*

Nick knew he would be a corpse by morning if Dawn's boyfriend caught him looking twice at her.

But Nick decided he wanted a girlfriend just like her.

✒️ **Read Proverbs 6:20–29. How are you lured into doing wrong?**

The toughest temptations you face nearly always have a face.

They have *cool* faces. You aren't tempted by a flea-infested drug dealer driving a beat-up car. A beautiful

105

girl or a gorgeous guy is harder to resist.

They have *caring* faces. They laugh at your jokes. They make you feel good. They think you're smart. They understand how you think and feel. They spend time with you.

In order to stay friends you're tempted to do whatever they want. You might think about throwing out God's commands—ranking on the class dork, joining in at the party, dating a non-Christian, blowing off school, or blowing up at your parents. It feels right when you think those faces are cool and caring.

But coolness isn't a perfect complexion or clothes or a car. And caring isn't making you feel right when you're doing wrong. In a warped way pimps care for prostitutes and people care for their dogs. That doesn't mean you want to be a hooker or a hound.

Who's cool? Who cares for you? People who guide you into wisdom, watch to protect you, and remind you to stay on God's paths.

When you walk, they will guide you; when you sleep, they will watch over you; when you awake, they will speak to you. For these commands are a lamp. . . .

PROVERBS 6:22–23A

45

Been There Done That

"Discussion ended," Paul's dad had announced. Paul crossed his arms and glared straight ahead.

As Paul's dad pulled the car to a stop at a red light Paul undid his seat belt and climbed out of the car.

"What are you doing?" his dad demanded. "Where do you think you're going?"

"I can't stand this. I'll walk home—if I decide to come home." The traffic light turned green. Cars honked. Paul's dad flipped on his hazard lights. Angry cars sped around.

"You don't understand me!" Paul shouted above the traffic noise as he walked away. "You don't know what I face!"

☛ **Read Ecclesiastes 1:9–10. Is the world you face different from what adolescents have faced in the past?**

You cringe when your mom offers to help you pick school clothes. Your dad dies a quick digital death whenever he tries to play video games. They both fear computers. Your four-year-old sister sets their digital watches and you have to program the VCR when they want to tape a show.

So when your parents tell you how to dress, what to listen to, who to hang out with, where to go, and when to be home, you're less than confident that they know what they're talking about.

Your parents don't go to your school. They may not have been born on this planet. But you can be sure that if the've lived on earth as long as you have, they understand at least a little of your world.

Even if your parents actually *were* born in the stone age they still understand trials and temptations. When they were younger they just got in trouble for different things—for not cleaning up the cave, driving the family dinosaur too fast, cutting their hair too short, or not piercing their nose.

There have always been opportunities to rebel against God. Everyone faces choices between right and wrong. There's nothing new under the sun.

. . . There is nothing new under the sun. Is there anything of which one can say, "Look! This is something new"?

ECCLESIASTES 1:9B–10

46

You Ain't Seen Nothin' Yet

"These are the happiest times of your life," people say.

You hope not.

In fact, you wish you could gleep over seventh grade. You started the year in a new school where you hardly knew anyone. You were laughed off your intramural basketball team. All your clothes fit funny. In December your orthodontist said you had to get braces—unless you wanted teeth growing out of your nose. Merry Christmas.

Speaking of your face—it doesn't look like it used to. You stare in the mirror, worried that one eye is lower than the other. Maybe your head is attached crooked.

Yesterday at church you dropped the offering plate—*KLANG KAjing gajing gajink*. This morning you had a major math test you forgot to study for. And then there's that beachball-sized zit on your chin.

If this is as good as life gets, then you dread what's ahead.

📖 **Read Psalm 84. How do you keep middle school cool?**

Ancient Israelites went to the temple in Jerusalem— the "house of the Lord"—to feel close to God. But they never had an easy walk. To stand in the splendor of

God's dwelling they dodged roadside thugs and endured dust, heat, and dryness.

Growing up is a trudge through the desert. God wants to mature your body, brain, and heart so that you look like Him (2 Corinthians 3:18). But on the way you're hot and bothered. You face new challenges at school. Sometimes you feel lonely. You struggle with changing relationships with your parents and friends.

You may like being a middle schooler. You may hate it. Either way, two things are true: It doesn't last long, and God helps you get along.

When the Israelites "set their hearts on pilgrimage," when they chose to live close to God, even the "Valley of Baca" (the valley of "weeping" or "thirst") became a well-watered oasis, a spread of palm trees and ponds. But the best was always yet to come. When the Israelites reached the temple they couldn't imagine a better place to be.

When you get to the end of your walk—and growing up God's way will take you the rest of your life—you'll look back and know you chose the right path. And you'll look around and know that you've come to the right place (Revelation 21:1–4).

Blessed are those whose strength is in you, who have set their hearts on pilgrimage. As they pass through the Valley of Baca, they make it a place of springs. . . .

PSALM 84:5–6A

Acknowledgments

Thanks to Lyn for sharing the fun of watching Nate and Kari grow, and to our parents, Roy and Lois Johnson and Tom and Pat Benson, for continuing to help us grow up.

Thank you to Gary and Carol Johnson and Bethany House Publishers for offering me new challenges and opportunities, and to Barb Lilland for good editing and encouragement on this series.

And thanks, most of all, to our Crossroads middle schoolers, parents, and ministry leaders and teachers for growing together during our five years of ministry at Elmbrook Church. You're the best!

Faithful Together Forever,
Kevin